lonely planet

KU-720-361

travellers' tips

Edited by Tom Hall

Travellers' Tips
1st edition – October 2003

Published by
Lonely Planet Publications Pty Ltd ABN 36 005 607 983

Lonely Planet offices
Australia Locked Bag 1, Footscray, Victoria 3011
USA 150 Linden St, Oakland, CA 94607
UK 72-82 Rosebery Avenue, London EC1R 4RW
France 1 rue du Dahomey, 75011 Paris

ISBN 1740596587

Text © Lonely Planet Publications Pty Ltd 2003
Commissioned in the UK
Printed through The Bookmaker International Ltd. Printed in China

Contents

chapter 1

itchy
feet

At the planning stage, think big. Round-the-world tickets mean almost anything is possible. You can always cut back your itinerary later, but the closer a big trip is to the trip of a lifetime, the more likely you are to make it happen.
Claire Marshall

Short of inspiration and ideas? It's very easy to encourage friends and relatives to bore you about their travels. Escaping when the photo albums come out may be harder.
Mark Gardner

Travel shows and fairs can be great sources of information. Go along: you can hear talks about destinations you may not have considered, and chat to major and smaller operators, equipment suppliers and publishers. There are often hefty discounts available.
Helen Smith

Your best buddy at home may not be the ideal travelling companion – you're going to be together all day every day for a long time. Before committing to going, try a long weekend away together to see if you're compatible.
Hamayan Ahmad

Thinking about working abroad? Give the competition some thought. From serving behind a bar to joining a yacht crew, your chances of getting the gig are higher if you've got the right skills.
Thomas Michael

Always shop around to get the best price on your flight. You can sometimes get good deals or free internal flights thrown in so think a little about what you are going to do before you book.
Imogen Franks

Get good insurance. No excuses.
Andy Lee

getting ready

Some level of culture shock is inevitable when you first arrive at your destination. The differences from home can totally blow you away, especially if you're unprepared. You can minimise this shock by reading up before you go and chatting to others who've been there.
Matt George

Always book your first night's accommodation when you're flying into a new country. You'll be tired, lost and often arriving at night. You can get slowed down waiting for luggage, with customs or getting into town. You'll really appreciate not having to search for a room.
Ashley Woodward

If you need to get a visa, find out what times the embassy or consulate is open and what documentation you'll need. Get there ahead of this time and be prepared to queue. This preparation will prevent you wasting days hanging around an embassy that's only open for an hour a week.
Jonathan Royle

Make sure that the company you book with is bonded to one of the travel regulatory organisations – normally ATOL or ABTA. Any company worth its salt will be able to answer your questions before you give it large sums of cash. Check also the terms and conditions in case you want to cancel or change anything.
Susan Aitken

Keep warm with multiple layers rather than bulky coats – these will annoy you extremely.
Jo Stein

Check if the countries you're travelling to require an International Driving Permit in addition to your domestic one.
Alex Anardis

Think very carefully about shoes. Nothing takes up space in your luggage like shoes.
Reagan

If you want to be really prepared, bring along a set of passport-sized pictures. These are good for visa applications, police reports if you get anything stolen and other unforeseen paperwork. You don't have to get new pictures every year, but think of how cheap they are back home and how much of a pain it will be to find a place to get them done at 3am in Nepal.

David Boyes

I email important details, such as passport, credit card, travellers cheques and insurance policy numbers, to my travelling email account. If I lose everything, I can still access this information. For those who worry about the security of Internet cafés etc, writing card and policy numbers in codes (for example consistently changing the last two numbers or inserting your phone number in the middle) will help keep the information disguised.

Carol Wiley

When your bags do go into limbo you'll be much happier if you've got a change of underwear, a toothbrush and a clean shirt in your hand luggage. Bags are rarely lost forever but they often go astray when you have tight connections or transfers.

Tony Wheeler

Expensive sunglasses and fancy watches will break and are obvious items for light-fingered people you meet on the road. Cheap ones will do the job and can be replaced without anguished gnashing of teeth and assault on credit card.
Nigel Dixon

Dress for the occasion – I think people who arrive in a country looking like tramps deserve it if they get put through hoops by the immigration officials.
Tony Wheeler

Learn some good travelling card games, like 'Shithead'. If you're not familiar with it, the first person you meet with a backpack on will be very happy to teach you!
Brian

Find out in advance if your visit coincides with festivals, carnivals or other events. If it does, you're in for a treat – but make sure you find a place to stay well in advance. Tourist offices and guidebooks are good sources of information.
Maureen Pace

upgrades, perks & tricks of the trade

Some budget airlines and travel agents have email newsletters that give breaking news on the latest fare deals. This is one way to get ahead of the rest in the scramble for the best flight prices.
Bruce Leonard

You are extremely unlikely to get an upgrade these days. You're more likely to get one if you dress smartly, ask politely and join the airline's frequent-flyer scheme. If you're genuinely on honeymoon or it's your birthday (or both), you could try that too. But don't expect one – airline staff have heard it all before, probably from the people ahead of you in the queue!
David Boyes

You'll always get a better deal on budget flights if you book online.
Harriet Courcey

There are a variety of cards you can get in advance that will get you all sorts of discounts – YHA, ISIC, Euro 26 and Senior Citizens cards are a few of them. Do some research, and flash them at every opportunity – even if you can't see any advertised deals, it never hurts to ask.
Tariq Samad

If you have all day to get somewhere, or you're in no hurry, take the bump if you are offered incentives to take a later flight. You can get cash, tickets, food vouchers, free hotels, phone cards and taxi vouchers in exchange. Cash is rare these days, but make sure you are confirmed on another flight, not just on standby, or you could be there for two days just for a cheap meal and a free ticket.
David Boyes

Take some water on the plane with you – flying is dehydrating and airlines often don't give you enough.
Chris Morris

If they say check in two hours early, listen to them. You have no idea how long the ticket queues, security or walk to the gate will be.
David Boyes

Go to the toilet before you get on any plane. If you don't think you have to go, go in and ask your body one more time if it is sure. Some flights require you to be seated during the 30 minutes of takeoff and landing. This includes no toilet breaks.
David Boyes

The best way to deal with an overly chatty passenger in the next seat is to fall asleep, preferably with headphones and eye mask on. If someone sitting next to you adopts this tactic, it doesn't necessarily mean you talk too much.
Paddy Guinan

If you're jet lagged and awake when the rest of the plane is snoozing, take a walk to the back of the plane. If the cabin crew are dozing too you can often help yourself to nibbles and drinks.
Paul Pike

Shave before you go through customs.
Jonathan

Many airport arrival areas have hotel booking desks which not only know what rooms are available and where, but also have the best last-minute rates. Singapore and Hong Kong airports are two good examples where you'll get a much better room rate at the airport than you would by just turning up at the hotel.
Tony Wheeler

When travelling with a suitcase, I always wrap a brightly coloured piece of material securely around the handle of the bag. It makes for easy and unmistakable identification even when many bags are coming through the carousel at once.
Carol Wiley

If you've got an expired driving licence or some similar photo ID, bring it along – it's safer than handing over something current when you have to provide a form of ID as security for a bike rental or similar.
Tony Wheeler

Some larger, international airports have minihotels within the terminal that can be a welcome relief for jet lagged passengers with a three- to four-hour wait until the next flight. Do a little research if you know you have a layover long enough to become horizontal for a while.
Vance Cox

Youth hostels and B&Bs may have fixed prices but hotels (particularly big ones) rarely have set rates. It's always worth asking if there is any special rate, weekend rate or whatever. The price you'll get quoted at the front desk – the rack rate – is always much higher than you'd pay through a travel agent or over the Internet.

Tony Wheeler

chapter 4

on the road

Be interested in whatever you do – a steel factory can deliver the goods if you let it.
Robert Reid

Don't shoot straight off the second you land with an ambitious itinerary. Take some time to relax and acclimatise or you may come home more strung out than when you went away.
Patrick Asprion

Ask to speak to the curator at a small museum or historical site. Often they'll be delighted to lead an interested (if not rare) visitor around, offering an insider's view of some otherwise dry and dated exhibits.
Robert Reid

When feeling disorientated on arriving in a foreign country, count to 10 before asking for advice. Staff in Foyles book-shop in London report breathless tourists, upon seeing inflatable globes hanging from the ceiling, asking if one is available for Britain.
Barney Andrews

Take care not to write off popular tourist sites as not worth a visit due to the crowds. There's a reason why busy places are as popular as they are. Visiting first or last thing (particularly if there is a late opening night) can help beat the mob.
Campbell Wright

Roll your clothes instead of folding them when you're packing. Less creases and more space!
Nick

If you're travelling with a friend or partner, split your stuff up between your packs to share the load.
Katherine

Rubber-soled 'action sandals' are great for keeping your feet ventilated. However, they are inadequate for serious outdoor activity. They're utterly useless at keeping pebbles and bugs out, and offer the top of your feet no protection.
Toto Ragnarsson

If you're doing trips of just a few days, leave the bulk of your luggage with your hotel and take a daypack with just essentials.
Katherine

On a bus, try to sit where you can see the luggage going on and off.
Monica

For your sanity and enjoyment, swift acceptance of your destination's levels of customer service, opening hours, punctuality and toilet culture is essential.
Samuel Vila

Wherever you go, make friends. If you make friends with other travellers you'll probably end up doing things you wouldn't otherwise have done and you may be offered a place to stay in the future. If you chum up with local people, they just might invite you over for dinner – a highlight of any trip.
Dayne Gedney

Make the most of good water pressure.
Lynette

For those who can't cope with washing their hair in cold
water, fill some large bottles up with water and leave them
in the sun all day. Make sure you are back before they
cool. You can then wash and rinse your hair in water of a
bearable temperature!
Linda Vickery

In hostels and budget accommodation, never ever look at
the colour of the pillow beneath the pillowcase. Take your own
pillowcase or two, and wrap the pillow up in those plus a
sarong or a towel. You need at least three layers of cotton
between you and the offending article. But never look – just
assume. And don't inspect the mattress too closely either.
Matt Casey

Calling home, checking your emails, beer and chocolate
are all great on-the-road pick-me-ups if you're feeling
a bit blue.
Sarah Haynes

If you're travelling with friends, make sure you plan some time apart. Do your own thing or you'll eventually want to kill each other. Not everyone wants to see that wax exhibition you've got your heart set on.
April Kilcrease

If travelling independently, wait before booking places to stay for the entire trip. After you've been somewhere for a few days, you'll get a feel for whether you need to call ahead to secure accommodation. You can decide at this point whether to cover your whole stay or just the next few nights, giving you more flexibility over your future plans.
Leo Groves

Swapping books with other travellers keeps your luggage down and at the same time exposes you to subjects you may not otherwise read.
Piers Swancombe

chapter 5

essential
kit

The Swiss Army are famous for one thing, and with good reason. Never leave home without a decent penknife.
Patrick Asprion

The sarong. I've used it as a bag, a curtain and a sunshade. I've worn it as a skirt (long or short), a scarf, a shawl and I've swum in it. Sometimes it's a towel, sometimes it's a blanket. I could even tear it into strips and use it as a bandage if I ever needed to. This is the one thing I take wherever I'm going.
Fiona Siseman

Duct tape, sometimes known as gaffer tape, is a wonder of the modern world. For the traveller, the uses are countless! It quickly and neatly repairs everything and anything such as torn backpacks, tents and shoes. It can also be applied to feet to prevent blisters, and won't come off easily.
Trayah Zinger

A world map is a great aid to on-the-road conversation, particularly when you have little common language with travelling companions.
Dennis Storey

Sealable plastic bags come in amazingly handy when backpacking. They're perfect for separating dirty and clean clothes, popping rain-soaked clothes into until they can be hung out to dry – a backpack full of damp clothes is not a good thing – and for storing muddy shoes so that your backpack interior is kept clean. Backpacking does not have to compromise your cleanliness!

Jennifer Mundy

When I have an item of clothing that is almost ready to be discarded, I put it aside to take on my long-distance bike trips. It's so much easier when you're on the road to just toss out those knickers with wimpy elastic than to wash everything. I do this with all items of clothing, usually at least 50% of my luggage. I also do the same with shoes and trainers. There's an added bonus – extra space for souvenirs!

Brenda White

Bring baby wipes. They can be used to replace toilet paper, napkins, paper towels, make-up remover, a sink, a bath or a shower. Not just for you, either.

Shawn & Sarah

Carry a fold-down bag. You'll often suddenly find yourself overloaded with unexpected purchases, gifts or acquisitions. This way you don't need to wreck your regular bag by overpacking it or have to buy a second bag. Mine folds down to about the size of a wallet.
Tony Wheeler

I always use film canisters, when I travel, to carry pills around – far less bulky and more waterproof than packets.
Anna Simon

Zip-off trousers give you the best of both worlds. Get a pair with plenty of pockets, combat-style, so you've got lots of places to put those need-to-have items.
Matthew

Safety pins! Use them as pegs to hang stuff from your pack, as substitutes for lost buttons, to pin a sarong around your bunk for privacy and to secure your sunhat in high winds. They also weigh practically nothing.
Magali Duchemin

Essential things to pack and carry with you are a smile and a sense of humour. Make sure you use them often, especially when things go wrong – you'll have much more interesting stories when you get back home!
Steff & Shaun

A small Maglite-style torch is a must for making your way across a darkened dorm but we all know they don't taste great when you hold them between your teeth. If you need two hands to rummage through your stuff, a sticking plaster wrapped around the thin end of the torch will save your teeth from cold hard metal.
Sue White

I take sticky notes with me and when I'm finished with a paperback or magazine, I just leave it where someone can find it but with a note clearly telling the world it's a free book.
Michael J Mallen

There will always be a snorer in a dorm room or a party next door to your private room, so take earplugs. Even if you never use them it's nice to know they're there.
Russell

A hardy, purpose-built flask is a much better bet than a plastic bottle of water – and much better for the local environment. It's easier to carry and will make you feel like a member of the foreign legion if you drink from it in the desert.
Susie Oldman

Always, always, always keep toilet paper with you.
Pat

money matters

Take half as much stuff and twice the money.
Bill Ethridge

Familiarise yourself with banknotes and exchange rates
as soon as you can upon arrival in a new country. Making
some mental rules about how much each note is worth will
stop you making mistakes when spending a new currency.
Colette Quinn

If you buy any expensive items, keep the receipts. You
may have to explain where that camera came from at an
internal customs check or when you leave the country.
Graham Parrish

Keep some small change in your pocket to avoid dipping
into a money pouch and exposing huge wads of cash every
time you want to buy an apple. If you're concerned about
security, cover the change with a wad of tissues.
Ed Drake

Put your funds on your credit card account so it's in credit to the tune of several thousand pounds. You can use this as a current account, maximising the number of outlets available to you. As it's your money, you often won't have to pay cash advance fees either.
Katrina Browning

Always confirm exactly how much car hire will cost and ask specifically about any possible extra charges.
Josh & Bec

If you really want to burn money use your hotel's laundry service or minibar or make a call (particularly an international one) on your room phone. There's always a cheaper alternative just down the road.
Tony Wheeler

If taking a taxi without a meter, it is a good idea to write down the fare agreed before the trip and get the driver to acknowledge it. If a higher fare is demanded later you can simply point to the piece of paper with the agreed fare and avoid any confusion.
Brendan Tarrant

Need money badly and none of the ATMs are accepting your credit card or bank card from back home? Go to the local casino. They make sure that anyone who wants to get at their hard-earned money can do so, no matter where they bank!
David Boyes

Look at prices with your group size in mind. It's remarkable how often a taxi for, say, four people can be cheaper than four bus or train fares.
Tony Wheeler

Always have a few US$1 notes on you – you can use them for changing small amounts of currency, small transactions and last-minute expenses, when the only other option is an ATM withdrawal or cashing a travellers cheque.
Timothy Drallop

Lots of museums and galleries have a free day each week or each month but quite often there are unannounced freebies as well, such as no admission charge in the last hour before closing.
Tony Wheeler

A full set of coins from each country you pass through is a cheap and very nice souvenir.
Kevin McKeon

Keep a close eye on your finances, get online banking and check the status of your funds often. There are emergency measures to get more funds to you but nothing will crush that wild and free spirit like finding you're broke 10,000 miles from home.
Folay Yeboah

Prices are lower in the sticks – cities, especially capitals, sap your funds like nowhere else.
Gwen Roberts

No matter how concerned you are about your son or daughter heading abroad, it's probably not a good idea to give them a credit card on your account.
Louie Maple

chapter 7

getting around

If it looks like you are going to get mobbed, ripped off or simply spooked by taxi touts as you leave the arrivals hall of the airport, walk around to the departures area and nab a taxi that someone has just arrived in. The atmosphere will be calmer and the driver more amenable to negotiation as he will be glad of a quick turnaround.
Brendan Tarrant

If you're sure it's safe, never pass up the opportunity to ride on the roof of a moving vehicle, and that includes a boat.
Reagan

When taking an excursion to a remote island or village, double-check return times – otherwise you may end up staying over or shelling out for an unplanned taxi or boat back.
Colette Quinn

If you do have to take a cab from the airport, ask at an information desk for a rough estimate of how much it should cost. While you are there, ask about the train or bus that can also take you to the city centre.
David Boyes

In many countries there is one day of the week when many museums and other attractions are closed (in Europe it's generally Monday). Think ahead: if you've got a big journey to do, that's the day to do it.
Matt George

Rail is by far the best way to travel in India, and watching the scenery is amazing. Make sure your train tickets are confirmed before you get on the train. Don't just take a vague head-shake as a yes or you might end up being thrown off the train in the middle of nowhere!
Kate Paddison

Avoid very long journeys. That two-day coach ride may look enticingly good value but, as you stumble off after 36 hours unable to take any more, you may wish you'd broken the trip.
Jesse Bonan

Get supplies that you enjoy eating before embarking on journeys of one or more days. Catering standards vary and a tin of pilchards may be a lifesaver on the Trans-Mongolian Railway.
Lauren Wright

At times you'll want to cover a lot of ground in a short time. Flights can eat into your funds but most regions and countries offer air passes that can keep the cost down. Often these have to be purchased before you go, so do your homework.
Stu D'Abernon

Have your destination written down in the local lingo and use it to check and double-check you've got the right bus or train. When there's only one bus a day this could avoid a big mistake.
Mario Vanetti

A bicycle is a cheap, environmentally friendly way to see a country at your own pace. The more you cycle, the less holiday weight you'll gain.
Will Stewart

chapter 8

close the
cultural gap

You don't have to be fluent in a language to speak it. Being able to say 'yes', 'no', 'please' and 'thank you' means you can speak the language – not much of it perhaps but enough to make a surprisingly big difference. It helps to be able to say 'one beer please' as well.
Tony Wheeler

Instead of pens, sweets or money, give kids you meet the gift of fun. Buy a bottle of bubble mixture and blow bubbles for them – they love it and it's healthy. Just watch out if there is traffic nearby when they are chasing the bubbles.
Meredyth Morgan

Respect the locals, especially when you're deciding what to wear for the day.
Anne

Churches and other religious buildings are great tourist sites, but they're still spiritual places – keep your voice down and check if you can take photos.
Ernesto

If you're looking for a place where you won't find other tourists, the best place to start is anywhere not listed in a guidebook.
Paula Golby

When museums and galleries and churches and temples tire you out, there's always the cinema. It's one of the most overlooked attractions in any foreign destination. There can be surprising discoveries in how movies are presented, how tickets are sold and how audiences react to risqué jokes – plus it's relaxing and normally pretty cheap.
Robert Reid

Some countries (most notably the USA) place more emphasis on tipping than others. A spot of people-watching over lunch will tell you if tipping is practised and help you to avoid any awkward situations.
Raph Abraham

Take some photos of your home and family. They help with homesickness and new-found friends like to see where and how you live.
Jo

Don't snub sports. Even if you couldn't care less, few places offer a less-guarded local scene than a rodeo or football game. Once at a minor-league hockey game in French Canada, I joined teens, mums and moustached dads pounding the low ceiling as 17-year-olds fought on the ice. It was better than the Louvre.
Robert Reid

Try to read a novel set in the area you're visiting.
Monica

If you say you're going to send a photo or an email to someone, make sure you do so – particularly if you've promised someone you've met while travelling.
Michelle

Wherever you go, you'll meet travellers who'll tell you how great this beach or that village was 10 years ago. The quicker you learn to ignore these people, the better trip you'll have. After all, they're still there!
Larry Hallegua

Haggling can be great fun, but don't get obsessed with it. Screaming yourself blue over 10p is not dignified nor worth the effort; nor will it make you an authentic 'traveller'. Let it go.
Carlos Rocha

Remember, karaoke is just as offensive in a foreign country.
Jason

solo travel

Travel light, travel faster.
Jol Ranger

An unexpected problem when travelling on your own is the
awkwardness of eating alone. Taking a book is a good way
to avoid feeling too conspicuous but make sure you don't
hide behind it. In many countries, you'll get plenty of offers
to join others.
Cliff Homerton

I make a point of seeking advice from books, websites and
other travellers on no-go areas of cities I'm visiting. I mark
these on my map with a highlighter before I go.
Trish Lotzer

A wedding ring is the best way to avoid unwanted amorous
attention.
Anna Hobson

When travelling alone to a sun-drenched spot, always make sure that you carry a spray version of sunscreen. The spray will cover all those hard-to-reach spots on your back and is easy to apply yourself.
Ronnie Munro

Large amounts of drink or drugs and being alone in an unfamiliar place are a bad combination.
Robin Jacks

Be careful of free drinks from strangers, they may be spiked.
Amanda

The less eye contact you make, the less risk of harassment – another use you may have overlooked for sunglasses.
Richard Magellas

Bag the top bunk for long train journeys – it's safer and there's a good chance you'll wake up in the night if anyone's trying to get at you or your gear.
Tommy Friar

You're less conspicuous travelling alone than in a big pack of tourists who make an obvious spectacle of themselves. You tend to blend in more when you are alone.
April Kilcrease

Unless you're trekking unaided to the South Pole, the only certainty of solo travel is that you're never on your own for long.
Ed Drake

chapter 10

shopping

Your bag doesn't have to expand until it's twice your weight. If you're on a round-the-world or long trip, think about tactically sending home items you don't need. Better still, be more selective about what you're picking up in the first place. That miniature mooning monk may look great in Milan station but will your parents really want to put it on the wall?
Tonia Pereira

You can always get a half-decent swimsuit at the airport.
Tera Chappel

If you're spending serious money, or setting your heart on something, check what paperwork, licences or taxes are needed. The last thing you want is to turn up at the airport with the buddha of your dreams only to be told you haven't got the right permit and have to leave it behind.
Morris Stephenson

If the country you're in uses bargaining, then bargain.
Kate

Ask local people to get an idea of market costs before shopping.
Gill Evans

Think twice before buying that beautiful antique from an unofficial source – you could be walking off with the contents of the local temple or church.
Robert Nunes

Try to buy your souvenirs from a needy local rather than a fancy shop or an expatriate hippy.
Sergio

There's no need to take CDs or lots of clothes to places like Thailand, Vietnam or Bali. It's cheaper and more fun to buy them there.
Pam Rybus

In countries where bargaining is the norm, the better dressed you are, the higher the starting price. If on a major buying spree dress down a bit.
Steff & Shaun

The best presents are sometimes simple things that can't be found at home – local football or rugby shirts and music by popular local artists for example.
Alex Newton

chapter 11

food

Splurge sometimes. You really can't get some of that stuff anywhere else. If everyone is chowing down on a big pastry from a certain shop, try one.
April Kilcrease

Get enough to share – hungry kids in your train compartment can make you feel very guilty about snacking away on your own.
Geoff Hall

A jar of peanut butter is a godsend. When travelling through Europe I tucked a container in my backpack as an afterthought and it was the best decision I ever made. All I had to do was buy bread and voilà – a whole meal!
Shannon Bell

Try the food, even if it still has teeth.
Brendan

You can find a perfect coffee almost anywhere. Grab one from any restaurant, sit back and relax. A spot of holiday smugness can do wonders for your appreciation of a new place. This also works with beer.
Darren Melsted

If vegetarian, learn how to say you are in the language of the country you're heading for to avoid confusion or unwanted food – it's easier to mime a chicken than broccoli!
Kris Kimola

Here's how to make free tomato soup: free ketchup packets, free milk for coffee, free hot water. Mix in free Styrofoam cup – and use your own personal flair!
Todd

Eating in lo-fi traveller-friendly cafés will nibble at your funds quicker than a mouse through a sack of grain. Get yourself down to the market and find out where the locals eat their lunches instead. It'll be a third of the price and a taste of real life.
Mike Evans

If you are going to eat from a street stall, avoid meat that's been sitting for a while or choose a busy place where they turn the food over quickly.
Melissa

Carry a packet of energy sweets (the ones with high glucose content) for those moments when there's no meal in sight and you or your companions are fading fast.
Imogen Franks

Going on a cookery course is great fun. It helps keep the memories of your trip alive and will make you very popular with friends when you return.
Bob Keenan

chapter 12

romance & nightlife

Everyone on the plane will know if you join the Mile High Club.
Dave Perry

Always, always, carry condoms. Aside from obvious reasons, different countries may have different sizes to what you're used to. If a friend is short of one you can earn a lifetime of free beer by being equipped. In emergencies, they can also add a layer of waterproofing to valuables when crossing rivers or caught in sudden storms.
Piotr Fijalowski

If you don't normally pull girls that good looking at home, make sure you're not in for any surprises when the clothes come off.
Jamie Snow

Whichever way your personal compass is pointing, make an effort to find out what's OK and, more important, not OK in the country you're visiting when looking for love on the road.
Malcolm O'Brien

Not picking up? Perhaps you smell, and haven't changed your shirt since Calais. Your scruffy, unshaven charm will only get you so far.
Matt George

Don't be too sad (or happy) if your fling ends with your flight home. Holiday romances are a lot harder to run away from than they used to be – email and cheap airfares can be good (and bad) things!
Pierre Dubois

Knowing how to claim to be gay or straight in the local lingo can ward off over-zealous approaches and can be adapted to suit individual situations.
Rachel Dodd

You don't have to dump your boyfriend or girlfriend if you go away without them. It can cement your relationship if it works. However, you'll probably discover quite quickly that long trips are more fun if you're single.
Lucy Cameron

Pick up free local papers and listings magazines. Even if you don't understand much of the language there should be enough to tell you where the best places are and what big acts are in town. Befriending hotel or hostel staff is another good way to pick up hints.
April Kilcrease

If you're joining a yacht crew, make sure it's very clear what your expected contribution is going to be. Some people are cool about swapping certain favours for free passage – you might not be.
Morris Stephenson

The hip crowd will often flit from bar to bar so don't get too comfortable in one place if you want to follow the beautiful people. Your great find at midnight might be closing up while everything's moved to the little place down the road you mistook for a library earlier.
Chrissy White

chapter 13
(unlucky for some!)

staying
safe

If travelling to a city you've never been to before, try to avoid arriving at night.
Luis

Other travellers are the best sources of information on pitfalls to avoid, and swapping tales and tips is a great icebreaker.
Maria Joseph

Get in the habit of tapping your pocket every few minutes to check for your stuff. Learn what your pocket feels like with your gear in it. This will help thwart pickpockets and give you peace of mind when you are shopping. If there are tons of tourists, count on tons of pickpockets.
David Boyes

Get a slim money belt that fits under your clothes. Put inside your passport, plane ticket, an emergency stash of cash, one small travellers cheque (if you're bothering to bring them) and your rail pass in sealable plastic bags. The bags are to protect everything from sweat. Stick those into the money belt and wear it. Never take it off except to shower. Even then make sure that it's within arm's reach.
April Kilcrease

Read up in advance about what you can and can't expect from your embassy. They can help in genuine emergencies but most of the time you're on your own. This is where insurance can come in handy.
David Boyes

If you're going drinking, map out the general area and which buses, subways or streets you'll need to take to make it back. Put this piece of paper somewhere you won't lose it. This makes stumbling home much easier.
April Kilcrease

Wear a helmet when scootering or motorbiking, even if it isn't the local custom. The wind in your hair may make your day, but rocks colliding with your head will make a holiday seriously less fun.
Jay Panayi

When setting your bag down, wrap the strap around the leg of your chair or your own leg if there's nothing else. This way you'll know if someone's trying to get into your things.
April Kilcrease

If you get robbed, report it as soon as possible and get documentation – you'll need it for insurance claims.
Alex

watch out!

Please don't buy any gems on the promise of reselling them on at a profit. If a deal seems too good to be true, it is!
Charles Marley

Don't hand over your credit card and bank account details unless you really have to. Get some documentation and keep receipts every time you do this.
Colette Quinn

Wait until you've got your luggage out of the boot of a taxi before paying the driver.
Jack Robinson

There are a few well-known tricks thieves use. Large groups of children crowding around you for no reason is often a cover for pickpocketing, as are distractions like spilling liquid on your shirt or stopping to ask you the time when you have no watch. Keep on your guard if anything suspicious happens.
David Boyes

Many countries you visit will have severe penalties if you're caught dabbling in drugs. In the long run, settling for getting drunk (if this is legal) may be a safer option.
Gav Byatt

Most people are robbed on the same day they change money. Put your cash away before you leave the booth or bureau, stay alert and make sure you're not being followed.
Gill Evans

Card-sharks, pool-hustlers, black-market moneychangers and offers of food and drink from strangers are just as dangerous as at home, if not more so when on the road. Keep your common sense and don't assume something is on the level just because your new friend is charming and convincing and you don't want to offend your hosts. Err on the side of caution at all times when it comes to money.
Matt Watson

If planning to take a popular excursion, ask to see would-be tour guides' licences. You don't necessarily have to move on if they don't have one but you may wish to adjust price and service expectations accordingly.
Francis Washington

If police or immigration officials are fining you for a seemingly innocuous offence or absence of paperwork, ask to see their ID and offer to accompany them to their office or the police station. Often this will be enough to discourage bogus operators.
Nick Jones

If you believed all you see in the travel press, you'd think that every backpacking destination was loaded with thieves, touts and scammers, just itching to relieve you of your backpack, camera or innocence. It just isn't so. I've had many run-ins with drug dealers, pickpockets and general ne'er-do-wells, and most of those have been in my home town. If you can survive the big city you flew out of, I guarantee you can survive the big city you're flying into. Use your common sense but don't let it become a blinker for new experiences.
Adrian Greenwood

family travel

When picking a destination, remember that countries with award-winning ice cream will hold fonder memories for children.
Henry Davis

Try to time flights to coincide with baby or toddler sleep times – this means early afternoon or evening flights.
Charlotte Hindle

Before departure, try and find a few stories, myths and legends about where you're going as bedtime story material. *Arabian Nights* for the Middle East and *The Jungle Book* for India can get kids interested and excited about an unfamiliar destination. This works for you too!
Dave Brook

Your child can sit in their buggy all the way to the departure gate – you do not have to leave it at the check-in. At the gate you'll have to fold it up and it'll be put on the plane at this stage. This makes pre-departure shopping and waiting so much easier.
Charlotte Hindle

Dusty, dull institution? Assure your loved one this is not the case and drag them inside that museum. At least in the developed world special effort is made to excite the younger generation. Elsewhere, a bit of advance planning will mean you can do this yourself. Torture, crime and disease from years gone by will generally enthral kids.
Emma Coney

The best time to travel is when a baby is still being breast-fed – fast, nutritional food, any time, which is easy to carry! If your baby has bottles then don't forget to take some washing-up liquid with you so you can thoroughly clean out the bottles at night-time in your hotel. Another good reason to travel with very small children is that they'll fit in a plane's sky-cot (if you remember to book it).
Charlotte Hindle

Make sure you ask about family rates. These may not be advertised everywhere and can help dramatically with costs.
Rob Simpson

A good tip for warming up your baby's bottle when you're in the middle of nowhere is to put it under someone's armpit for half an hour.
Charlotte Hindle

There are very few places you can go in the world where kids aren't loved and where yours won't be treated like royalty. Travelling as a family will open doors to parts of society you'd never see as a couple.
Jo Miller

In Europe there are lots of hotels which have swimming pools but which are still pretty cheap. A swimming pool makes a huge difference to any child's enjoyment of a trip and is well worth any extra euros you'll spend. Also, don't forget to look out for hotels with baths rather than showers – the under-threes hate showers and really miss the bath-time routine. And remember to book non-smoking rooms – smoking ones can smell really foul regardless of how clean they are.
Charlotte Hindle

If travelling with the very young, bring any must-have food, nappies or medicine with you. Similar goods are available but they're not necessarily identical and you may not want to risk irritation.
Philip Barr

As we travel a lot, I always keep a fully packed suitcase for our children. By this I mean all I ever have to add is clean clothes. All their first-aid stuff, medication, vitamins, travel toys, favourite foods which you might not get abroad (like jars of Marmite and Rice Krispies), swimming costumes etc, remain packed at all times. So much thought goes into what children might need when they're abroad that I couldn't bear to unpack and re-pack for every trip.
Charlotte Hindle

Life will be easier for everyone if you practise bargaining. A ratio of two boring old churches to one trip to the funfair is about right.
Jim Oxley

Kids and business hotels don't mix and, come to think of it, what are you doing in one on holiday?
Lizzy Ayton

Always take both a pushchair and a baby-carrying back-pack. This gives your youngster a lot of variety when out and about. If they feel like being up high, seeing everything and really participating in life abroad then the baby-carrier is best. For sleeping or quietly absorbing a foreign culture the pushchair is the best place for them.
Charlotte Hindle

Stock up on kids' essentials before leaving a big town if you're heading off the beaten track. Halfway along the Kokoda Trail is not the best place to run out of wet wipes.
Samuel Vila

Hydrated and non-sunburnt children are more likely to be happy. Lashings of water, lots of sun cream and less exposed skin should top your parental to-do list.
Lawrence Smith

Bored of your parents' stories about how wonderful Sydney was 30 years ago? Shut them up by suggesting they relive it – this time with you in tow. Don't knock it, they may pay!
Jen Fearn

health

If you have prescriptions, make sure you are up to date before you go. Any relevant paperwork to pick up extra supplies abroad is a must for your valuables wallet.
Sam Hadari

Don't miss out on jabs to save money – it may seem a lot to pay but it's preferable to getting very ill. Many jabs last for several years so if you're a frequent traveller you won't always need to get them all.
Lal Bellari

A first-aid kit should be the first item in your pack. Hopefully you won't need to open it but it may prove the most crucial thing you pack. Remember to customise it according to your destination.
Justin Barlow

Most people go to the doctor's before a trip but a visit to the dentist is equally essential. You may find yourself a long way from a modern, comfy surgery with goldfish and magazines, and your gums may regret it.
Harriet Cracknell

Iodine-flavoured water beats dysentery.
Helen

Stay away from ice in drinks in developing countries. It may cause a moment of offence but it could save you from a dose of the trots.
Jesse Bonan

The best way to avoid getting nasty insect-borne diseases is to not get bitten. If in areas with a risk of infection, keep your arms and legs covered in lightweight and light-coloured cool clothing – and don't forget the long socks. These rules apply when sleeping too.
Colette Quinn

You'll always see the funny side of last night's diarrhoea in the morning. Your travelling companions may not take that long.
Matt George

Check the seal on bottled water. It's not unheard of to find tap water where you're not expecting it.
Frank Mills

keeping
in touch

Internet birthday cards are an easy way to keep your family and friends back home happy with you.
Thomas

Letters are still more appreciated than emails for non-urgent communication.
Helen Owen

Remember, the cheapest Internet access is often the slowest.
Kyle Hopkins

Mobile phones are an unnecessary item to take on the road and they may tie you to home in ways you come to dislike. If you have to bring one with you, check it has roaming and will work where you're going. Some countries work on a different frequency and your phone will simply not function when you get there. Of course, I'm not suggesting for a moment that this may be an excuse to avoid keeping in touch apart from when it suits you!
Evan Peters

Reading the local press is a great way to connect with your destination and keeping an eye on the international news section will connect you to the real world. Don't come back saying 'Osama who?'
Alison Manning

Making your own website can be a better way to keep people up to speed with what you're doing than sending heaps of emails.
Jenny

Search out poste restante addresses before you go. It's amazing how a few letters from home can make your day. It's also really nice to feel that you're following a time-honoured travelling tradition. Get your favourite magazine sent for that welcome taste of home.
Hannah Warwick

Don't put that credit card in a payphone, even for a quick call home. It's a hugely expensive way to call.
Simon Napier

Agreeing a check-in time each week can save a lot of concerns with the folks back home.
Nick Jennings

If you find yourself in one of the few places in the world without Internet cafés, once you've pinched yourself it should be easy to find a communications centre where you can call or fax.
Janie Brotherton

Even if you travel internationally with a mobile, use a phone card. You can then make the international call at calling card rates rather than at the usually sky-high roaming charge. You just pay (on your mobile) for the local call.
Tony Wheeler

Check local libraries for Internet access. It's usually cheaper and sometimes free.
Ross

capturing
the moment

A diary of your trip will bring back more vivid memories than photos. You get plenty of opportunities to sit down and write, which doesn't happen at home. As you take more trips, the library you build is a great memento of where all that money went!
Charlie Hunter

If you take a camera, document your trip, not history. Photograph the now of a place rather than landmarks – that means billboards, traffic police, cars and taxis, fashion, locals, tourists queuing, pavement cafés. Get as many people in shots as you can – including you and people you meet. It'll be more meaningful later.
Robert Reid

Telling travel stories at home doesn't mean boring your friends to tears. Bringing in souvenirs and even sound effects (a dictaphone won't take up much space in your luggage) at the right moment can rescue you from losing your audience.
Matt George

Consider leaving a camera at home. How much energy and stress have we wasted on getting the right photograph that invariably ends up too dark or bleached? Friends and family back home are never as interested in our trips as we'd like them to be. Take a sketch-pad instead.
Robert Reid

If you're going abroad to snap wild animals, a trip to your local zoo can familiarise you and your camera with your subject matter.
Lee Brighting

If you're looking for some extra cash, write some travel articles for the local tourist newspapers. Take some relevant photos too – you'll get paid more for articles with pictures.
Jol Ranger

Journal advice: document the mundane, don't be tempted to create overarching, macro-political revelations that no-one will want to read and you'll be embarrassed by later. The best journal is for personal use, to conjure up some key moments in a trip that will trigger more memories. Keep it simple, fragmentary and ordinary.
Robert Reid

Ask permission before taking photos of people: if they refuse, don't snap anyway. Be prepared to pay a small fee.
Stef Bollina

Travelling with a partner? Why not share a camera and get two sets developed at the end? You'll find you end up taking a lot of similar shots and, in some cases, who gets the best images can become a source of friction between companions.
Sam Lane

Always carry a spare battery for your camera – some are hard to come by away from home and you don't want to find yourself miles from the nearest shop with the perfect shot and no battery.
Imogen Franks

When developing film on the road you get what you pay for. Ask at camera shops for their recommendations. If prints become cumbersome you can always send them home – but think about either hanging on to negatives or mailing them separately.
David Briggs

chapter 19

coming home

If you're feeling homesick to the point where you're making everyone around you miserable, don't be scared to go home. You're meant to be broadening your horizons and having the time of your life. If you're hating every minute it may just not be for you.
Alex Williams

To avoid ridicule, the facial hair you have lovingly cultivated really should be shaved off on the last day of your trip.
Tom Hall

Though your friends and relatives may be thinking of a big homecoming, if you think it might be the last thing you need after three months in the rainforest and a two-day journey home, say so. Better to make your own way back than freak out upon seeing your nearest and dearest for the first time and upset everyone.
Hilary Bolan

If being at home is starting to feel like the worst thing ever, do something you missed when on the road – wander down to your local for a game of pool, take a hot bath when you want to, hop on your beloved bicycle for a spin. Home comforts can compete with on-the-road thrills in subtle ways.
Mal Southwick

Make sure you stick your photos in an album or scrapbook and type up your stories. You can add ticket stubs, postcards and anything else you picked up on the way. In the months and years after getting home you'll be glad you did.
Matt George

Don't be surprised if your travel stories are greeted with at best indifference and at worst boredom and jealousy by your pals. Short-circuit the frustration – like-minded souls in clubs like Globetrotters and online travel bulletins and news groups want to hear about your travels. You could also put your experiences to good use and set up a website to pass on your photos, yarns and wise words to the world.
Jane Wiseman

Planning your next trip is a great way to banish the blues. Even a virtual holiday can make you an expert on global affairs and a valuable player in pub quizzes. You'll also never be short of ideas for next time.
Philippa Hughes

Keep in touch with friends you made on the road. Letters, emails and phone calls will bring back happy memories and hopefully lead to more travels in the future.
Michael Mansfield

chapter 20

never
thought
of that

In most tropical countries, limes are cheap and good to carry in your bag. They are healthy to eat (full of Vitamin C) and taste great squeezed into water. They are antiseptic (you can clean cuts with them if you can bear it) and make a great natural wet wipe rubbed on hands. They're ideal for those long bus journeys when it's difficult to wash.
Graham Williams

Don't write off flatlands until you've seen them. Get in the middle of it, surrounded by swaying wheat and out of view of roads, and majesty pours. If you're driving through flat landscapes, detour on to a side-road towards a near horizon, one that ends a mile or so away. Often it means the ground drops unexpectedly offering a view as stunning as from a mountain top, without anyone else there to gawk with you.
Robert Reid

Lifting a fully loaded pack onto your back isn't as easy as it sounds, but you have an inbuilt tool to make it easier – your foot! Try this: rest your pack on the ground next to your right foot, holding the right shoulder strap in your hand as if you're about to put your pack on. Then, as you lift your pack up with your arm, hook your toes underneath the bottom of the pack and give it a flick, pushing the pack up and onto your back with ease.
Sue White

Stay with old family friends and steal their toothpaste when you leave.
George Dunford

Everyone says take photocopies of your passport, tickets etc. Fair enough, but I say photocopy them onto acetate sheets so that they can't get soggy and useless!!
Mike Evans

Need to check the weight of your luggage for the flight home? Make a set of scales out of a coathanger, two shopping bags and one-litre water bottles. Hang the coathanger. Tie one bag to each end. Place full water bottles in one bag. A full one-litre bottle weighs 1kg. Place a bundle of your gear in the other bag and adjust until the coat-hanger hangs level. Do this as many times as necessary to weigh out all your gear and simply add up the total weight!
Pamela Hagedorn

To keep a bar of soap from falling apart and getting really disgusting, throw it into a stocking. Cut the stocking off with just a little extra length and throw the whole package into a plastic bag or soap container. Your soap will last forever. Bring an extra stocking or two if you're going to be out for the long haul, they weigh nothing and take up no space.
Jake Hansen

When I go trekking and have limited water I wash my hands by taking a big gulp of water and using my mouth like a tap. The water is easily directed, has an adjustable supply rate and slakes the thirst – and you don't waste anything!
Fred Preston

After being on the road alone for a while, you'll probably start to value your freedom and solitude. Claiming to be a chronic snorer is a good way to avoid sharing a dorm or room with an irritating fellow traveller. If you find a couple attach themselves to you, sleeping with one of them is a good way to shake them both off.
Georgina Green

One time while hiking my girlfriend was getting a blister on the side of her foot, so I grabbed a clump of soft green grass and put it between her sock and shoe. She looked a bit odd, with grass hanging out of her shoe, but it helped – and her foot smelled like a freshly mowed lawn.
Bonnie Byrne

I highly recommend night-vision goggles to anyone planning on staying in dorm rooms and having to get up and out before the sun rises. With night-vision goggles it will be possible to check under the bed for any stray articles without having to turn on the light and disturb your fellow travellers.
Marissa Binstock

If you need to know direction at night and you don't have a compass...oh, and if you're in a slightly populated area...you can still figure out your directions without prying the moss off all the trees. Basically, look around at where people's satellite dishes are pointing. If you are in the northern hemisphere they will be pointing south. If you are in the southern hemisphere, they will be pointing north.
Tammy Fortin

Empty film canisters make ideal shot glasses for drinking games!
Alison Kemp

Old jogging bottoms have a multitude of uses. Cut off at the knee to make a pair of shorts. Cut off the lower leg and use as hand muffs to keep both your hands warm with one leg – at night they can keep your feet warm. Break the elastic around one ankle and use as a neck warmer or hat. Tie at one end to close and use as a pouch to keep food up a tree at night so bears can't get to it. At Christmas, you can hang it up for Father Christmas – far bigger than your average stocking.
Ed Pickard

When hitchhiking in Japan, a sign saying 'wherever the wind blows me' won't help you get a ride, but people will stop to take pictures of you.
Bill Fink

Travelling through hottest Africa and want a cold beer?

1. Put a can in your wet sock.
2. Tie it to the tree.
3. Drink cold beer.

The wind (even if it's gentle) will surprisingly make the beer get cooler.
Andy James